MY **WORK**BOOK

HOW TO FIND A JOB—**EVEN DURING TOUGH TIMES**—AND SURVIVE YOUR FIRST YEAR IN THE WORKPLACE

ZELDA FREUD

New York

MYWORKBOOK
How to find a job—even during tough times—
and survive your first year in the workplace

ISBN 978-160037-573-6 (paperback)

Published by:

MORGAN · JAMES
THE ENTREPRENEURIAL PUBLISHER
www.morganjamespublishing.com

Morgan James Publishing, LLC
1225 Franklin Ave. Ste 325
Garden City, NY 11530-1693
Toll Free 800-485-4943
www.MorganJamesPublishing.com

Cover Art and Illustrations by Yuko Shimizu www.yukoart.com
Cover and Interior Design by Sarah Mangerson sarahmangersondesign@mac.com

To every twentysomething looking for a job or starting a terrifying, but exciting chapter in life: *work*. And to one person in particular, my husband, who constantly pushes me to do more and do better and who has inspired me by his passion, drive, and determination.

"Never, never, never give up."

—Winston Churchill

"This is our moment. This is our time, to put our people back to work and open doors of opportunity for our kids; to restore prosperity and promote the cause of peace; to reclaim the American Dream and reaffirm that fundamental truth, that, out of many, we are one; that while we breathe, we hope. And where we are met with cynicism and doubts and those who tell us that we can't, we will respond with that timeless creed that sums up the spirit of a people: Yes, we can."

—President Barack Obama's Acceptance Speech
November 4, 2008

CONTENTS

ACKNOWLEDGMENTS

A big thank you to Tamara Dews, Etty Lewensztain, Erin Corrigan, Robert Rostron, and Emanuele Grimaldi for believing in this project, and sharing your experiences and insights with me. Thank you to all the young associates at RF|Binder: you have inspired me throughout the writing of this book. Thank you to Shara Grossman for your precious help. And, finally, a very special thank you to my supportive and loving family.

INTRODUCTION

Finding a job and settling into the first year in the workplace are definitive phases in the life of a twentysomething. When I reflect on these phases, I think of accomplishment, freedom, independence, teamwork, first apartment, new friends, and fun, but I also think of hard work, long hours, blackberries, mastering multitasking, and deadlines.

The first year as a professional entails a demanding lifestyle and a new approach to working, very different from all your previous experiences. Many of you will leave your parents' home or dorms and find a place on your own or with roommates. You will receive your first real paycheck, which will mean more money, but also more expenses. After years of following your own schedule, you will be catapulted in a world of calendars and time management. Vacation time will have to be requested well in advance, and it will only be a very limited time off compared to that enjoyed in the college years. Also, the frequent and concrete feedback that you received in college from grades and teacher's comments will be replaced by infrequent and vague remarks. In fact, it will take lots of initiative from you to actually seek out constructive feedback and advice from your superiors.

The first year in the working world is an important year. It is a time to build the foundation of your career. You will find out what your strengths are, what you really enjoy doing, and what needs improvement. It's a year of change. You will start to affirm yourself, to come out of your shell. You will have many highs and lows. At work, the first few weeks will be terrifying, but also exciting. Everything will be new. Then, the honeymoon phase will arrive. Work will be manageable; people will be nice and friendly. It's the learning period, so expectations are low. Then, one day, your to-do list will just start growing; your boss will start sending you more and more requests. Deadlines will be shorter, and your time in the office will definitely seem longer. You will feel overwhelmed and tense. You will start thinking about work a lot. This will make you nervous, but it's a positive sign. It means people are starting to trust you, to give you more responsibilities. Work will be more challenging, which means that you will have more opportunities to grow professionally. Don't give up. Things will get better once you get accustomed to the new expectations.

MYWORKBOOK will guide you through the challenges and doubts of your job search, and it will offer tips and insights on how to succeed in (and survive) your first year on the job.

The Q&A section covers topics that are particularly challenging for recent college graduates—from the job search to the actual first year of work experience. My everyday work as an HR manager has helped me develop the 20 Q&As. The young adults who come in for interviews, the résumés I receive, and the twentysomethings who work in my agency and who have gone through all the challenges outlined in this section have inspired me throughout the writing of MYWORKBOOK.

The interview section is an additional resource for college graduates entering the workforce. Five very different professionals—from a Gen Yer to a baby boomer—have expressed their opinions and shared their insights on how to best leverage a young adult's first working experience. As you will notice, the interviewees discuss many of the topics covered in the Q&As. The two sections complement each other very well.

With the state of the current market and the uncertainty of what's going to happen next, it is more important than ever to submit high quality résumés and cover letters during your job search, and to work even harder to make sure nothing is falling through the cracks as you start your first working experience. You will be facing a highly competitive job market. Therefore, this is a time for you to show all of your talents and to also keep your antennas always active so that you can be receptive to any new information, ideas or suggestions.

I hope MYWORKBOOK can bring the best out of you and make you shine like a star during interviews, career fairs, networking gatherings, and, finally, at *work*!

1. How do you create a résumé that gets you noticed?

Take a look at your résumé and ask yourself the following question: would you still be interested in reading it if it wasn't your own? Remember, your résumé is your business card—it represents who you are, at least accomplishment-wise. Therefore, you should not underestimate the task of creating a résumé. It will take time to make it smart, straightforward, and sleek, but the extra effort will go a long way.

You can see big results by following these six tips:

- Spell-check carefully. Computer spell-check programs don't always pick up on spelling and grammar errors, so proofread it yourself, and ask your friends and family to look it over as well. Attention to detail is the #1 rule for a successful résumé.

- Organize your résumé by inserting information in reverse chronological order: your most recent academic accomplishment should be at the top. Likewise, your most recent internship should be at the top of your professional experience. Remember to always include dates.

- Set up your résumé for easy reading: use a standard font such as 11 or 12 point Times New Roman or Arial. Bold, italicize, or underline important headlines (i.e. bold the name of the company you interned with; italicize your job title). Use bullets to separate accomplishments.

QUICK TIPS

- Attention to detail—spell-check carefully.
- Organize information in reverse chronological order.
- Use a standard font.
- Use simple language and short sentences.
- Focus on accomplishments over tasks.
- Ask for feedback.
- Be concise—one page maximum.

- Use simple language and short sentences. Leave out the articles "a," "an," and "the," and the pronouns "I," "me," and "myself."

- Accomplishments, accomplishments, accomplishments. Focus your résumé on accomplishments, not tasks. Responsibilities and duties are important, but your successes are the ones that will set you apart.

- Finally, ask for a fresh perspective. Ask as many people as you can in your network (i.e. career service advisors, family members, former internship colleagues) to look it over and give you feedback.

Résumés sent to hiring companies are very often overlooked because many applicants don't follow the above suggestions. Now, more than ever, you need to stand out from the crowd. A concise and punchy résumé—not more than one page long—and a well-written cover letter will increase your likelihood of landing a face-to-face interview.

2. How can you make your cover letter shine?

HR departments receive hundreds, sometimes thousands, of cover letters per year. The majority are poorly written and uninteresting. Yet a cover letter is your chance to really market yourself to a potential employer, and a well-written one can single-handedly land you a job interview.

By following these simple tips, you should achieve success in this crucial phase of your job search:

- Address your cover letter to a real person. Do your best to find out the name of the HR manager at the hiring company. "To whom it may concern" and misspelled names are bad ways to start a cover letter.

QUICK TIPS

- Address the cover letter to a real person.
- Start with a punchy sentence.
- Don't repeat your résumé.
- Write down what makes you special.
- Use words that show enthusiasm.
- Use simple language and uncomplicated sentences.
- Be concise—one page maximum.
- Request an interview.
- Proofread and ask for feedback.
- Follow up—be politely persistent.

- Start your cover letter with a punchy first sentence to really grab the attention of the reader.

- Use your cover letter to highlight the aspects on your résumé that are relevant to the position. However, don't repeat your résumé. Present your skills and knowledge in terms of how hiring you will benefit the company.

- Stand out as a candidate. It could be your GPA, a particular major, a fabulous internship, or a foreign language competency (if relevant to the job opening). Write down what makes you special.

- Use words that show enthusiasm for the position and the organization. Search for the company's website and incorporate what you find in the letter.

- Use simple language and uncomplicated sentences. Be concise, clear, and straightforward. Never write more than one page.

- Request an interview. "I would greatly appreciate the opportunity to come in and meet with you at your earliest convenience," is a smart approach.

- Proofread the cover letter yourself, and ask as many people as you can to look it over as well. As with your résumé, attention to detail is the #1 rule for a successful cover letter.

- Finally, follow up religiously by email or telephone. If the position has been filled, ask for an informational interview. The objective is for the hiring manager to put a face to your name and to eventually contact you when a position opens up. Remember, always stay in touch. Be politely persistent.

"Why should I interview this person?" is the question HR managers ask themselves while reading cover letters. Take the time to carefully craft your letter so that it answers this question.

3. How do you job hunt in cyberspace and make your professional information available online?

As a job hunter in the electronic age, it's important to be savvy when it comes to online tools that will help you find your first job.

- First of all, make your online résumé keyword-rich. Search through job postings within the industry you are interested in and look for common terms. Make sure those words are in your résumé.

- Post your résumé on online career websites, such as Yahoo!HotJobs, monster.com, or careerbuilder.com. Recruiters may see your résumé—chances are higher if your résumé is keyword-rich—and contact you as a result. In addition, once you have your résumé in a job database, it's simple to submit it to employers that post their jobs on the site. Be sure to continually update your online résumé. You can also store numerous versions of your résumé, allowing you to select the most relevant one to send.

- Visit the websites of companies you are interested in. Although you might not find an entry-level job opening, send a résumé and cover letter to the company expressing your desire to be considered for future jobs.

- If you have submitted your application online, follow up within a week of submitting your materials. Many résumés get lost in cyberspace, and, more importantly, you want to reaffirm your interest in the position.

- Post your résumé on social networks, such as LinkedIn, Facebook, or Doostang. Recruiters are all over these sites, proactively searching for potential hires. Then, get social! Join common-interest network groups, or connect with professionals through discussion forums. Even talking to your fellow classmates about their future career plans can be a big networking tool.

QUICK TIPS

- Make your online résumé keyword-rich.
- Post your résumé on online career websites.
- Continually update your online résumé.
- Be proactive: send your résumé and cover letter to all companies that interest you.
- Follow up within a week to reaffirm your interest.
- Post your résumé on social networks.
- Get social—join groups and discussion forums.
- Be smart about your virtual profile—remove unsuitable pictures or text.
- Use all of your resources.

- Remember that nowadays recruiters are not only using Google and Yahoo to conduct background checks on candidates, they are also looking up applicants on social network sites, such as the ones listed above. Be smart about what you post:

  – Remove photos or text that could be considered inappropriate by potential employers.

– Keep your personal information private: apply settings that limit access to your pages.

It would be regrettable to lose a job opportunity because of an inappropriate virtual profile. Unsuitable pictures or comments posted on social networks such as MySpace or Facebook are considered an indicator of a person's poor decision-making ability. So be smart, and don't let things posted on the Internet come back to haunt you!

Job hunting online is one of many strategies you can use to find your first job. Use all of your resources, and combine a variety of approaches, such as attending career fairs and reaching out to family, friends, alumni services, professional and industry associations, and former internship colleagues.

CAREER WEBSITE	COMPANY/CONTACT NAME

JOB TITLE	RESUME SENT	FOLLOW UP

4. How to make the most out of career fairs?

Career fairs are great places to find out about positions with potential employers, to obtain company and industry information, and to distribute résumés.

In order to make the most out of your career fair experience

- Conduct preliminary research on the companies you are most interested in. The more you can communicate with the organization representative, the more unforgettable you will be.

- Bring numerous copies of your résumé. Put your résumé on nice, cream-colored résumé paper.

- Arrive with a one-minute summary of who you are and what you have to offer to the employer. Practice with as many people as you can before the fair. Demonstrate confidence, enthusiasm, and energy. Remember, this is not a face-to-face interview. Many other people are waiting to speak with the company representative; therefore, speak concisely and clearly.

- Be ready to ask a few smart questions about the position and about the company in general.

- Manage your time effectively. Talk to every company that fits your experience and interests.

- Dress to impress. Whether you are a young man or a young woman, business suits are the best choice.

- Remember to get the interviewers' business cards. You will then be able to send your cover letter and résumé to them directly.

- Make sure you know how to apply for available jobs. Follow the recruiters' instructions as quickly as possible.

- Follow up with a thank you letter. Sending a handwritten thank you note is a great way to stand out from the crowd and be remembered.

QUICK TIPS

- Conduct preliminary research on the companies you are most interested in.
- Bring several copies of your résumé.
- Prepare a one-minute summary of who you are and what you have to offer.
- Demonstrate enthusiasm and confidence.
- Speak concisely and clearly.
- Ask smart questions.
- Dress to impress.
- Get the interviewers' business cards and send them your résumé/cover letter.
- Follow instructions on how to apply for available positions.
- Follow up—send a handwritten thank you note.

5. How do you establish a good network and build relationships?

Building and maintaining relationships is one of the keys to success, not only in the early stages of your career, but throughout your work life. Therefore, while job hunting, it is not enough to reach out only to potential employers. You have to reach out socially as a job seeker. How do you do this?

- First of all, network with your family and friends. Be proactive about it, and ask them to think about contacts that might be useful. Friends and family are great resources to start building relationships.

- Your college career center and alumni associations are also useful resources. Even your high school can be a good source of network opportunities if it has an alumni association.

- Reach out to former internship colleagues/employers. Hopefully you have stayed in touch with them. However, even if you haven't, send them an email or give them a call, and ask for their help.

- Professional and industry associations can be the key to a shorter job search. First of all, if you are part of an association, add it to your résumé under professional/industry affiliations. That name is often used by recruiters while searching through the Web for candidates. Second, check the associations' events listings, and participate fully. These are fabulous ways to meet people, discuss your experience and interests with professionals, and collect business cards. At first, you might feel uncomfortable or shy not knowing anyone else there. Just remember that everyone at these events was in your shoes at one point in their lives, so don't panic; be positive, friendly, and polite.

QUICK TIPS

- Network with your family and friends.
- Network with your college career center and alumni associations.
- Reach out to former internship colleagues/ employers.
- Participate in professional and industry associations' events.
- Use as many resources as you can i.e. local chamber of commerce and the business press.

- Finally, use other resources, such as your local chamber of commerce. Ask for a member directory, and send out your résumé and cover letter to companies that interest you. Also, take a look at business press. *Forbes*, *Fortune*, and *BusinessWeek* magazines collect a list of the largest employers in the United States every year. Use these lists as additional resources to find a job.

Remember, the key to establishing a powerful network of people is to make acquaintances outside of your own social world. By doing so, you allow yourself to gain a variety of opportunities to find out about new jobs and to collect new information and ideas. So get out there!

6. If you can't find a job, should you pursue an internship? How do you turn an internship into a full-time position?

As you know, completing several internships during your college career increases your chances of getting a job. You will not only discover your likes and dislikes career-wise, but you will also enter the job market with an impressive background and valuable experience. Moreover, employers often hire directly from their internship programs.

If, for one reason or another, you haven't completed any internships during your college years or none of the internships lead to a full-time position you desired, it might be interesting to choose an internship as a starting point to getting a full-time job, particularly in a tough job market like the current one.

- Demonstrate your skills and work ethic.
- Show that you are versatile.
- Be a team player.
- Establish a strong relationship with your manager.
- Network through the company.

Below are some tips on how to turn this internship into a full-time job offer:

- If the company you are interning at is actually your ideal workplace, then you will have to find ways to stand out.

– Make an extra effort to demonstrate skills and work ethic: take on all types of tasks and prove that you are a hard worker and a valuable asset to the company.

– Show that you are versatile and that they can count on you to do many things at the same time.

– Be a team player. Be friendly, polite, and positive with everyone. Learn from your co-workers and supervisors. Listen and ask questions.

– Establish a strong relationship with your manager. Make his/her life easier by meeting his/her needs, contributing with fresh ideas, and demonstrating dedication and commitment to the tasks on hand.

– Network through the company; don't be afraid to approach people you'd like to meet, but don't be overly persistent. Approach them during lunchtime or at the end of the day, when things might be less hectic.

- If the company you are interning at is not your ideal workplace, think of it as a starting point to gain new skills and network. You will come into contact with many individuals who may have valuable connections and can help you land your first job. Therefore, work hard and keep your eyes and ears open at all times.

7. How do you stand out from the crowd both in a job interview and in the follow-up?

There are several things that you can do to prepare for an interview.

- First of all, do some research. Search for the company's website and learn about the firm's philosophy, clients, and services. Take it further, and do some research on the search engines about the company. Look for articles mentioning the CEO or a specific department. While you research, prepare questions to bring to the interview. Demonstrating interest in the company and asking smart questions will set you apart.

- Prepare a nice folder with copies of your résumé and writing samples and bring it to the interview.

- Dress appropriately. Whether you are a young man or a young woman, business suits are the best choice.

- During the interview, sell your skills and your know-how to the potential employer. Remember though, you are looking for your very first full-time job, so don't be full of yourself! Remember to present your skills and knowledge in terms of how hiring you will be beneficial for the company.

- Be knowledgeable, friendly, and positive. Ask questions about the organization, its culture, the working environment, and how is it different from other companies. Learn more about the position that has to be filled—the skills needed, the responsibilities involved, and the expectations.

- Following the interview, thank you letters are not only appreciated, they are expected. In these relatively short emailed or handwritten letters, reaffirm what you liked about the company, add new insights by using the information you acquired during the interview, and express how your skills will meet the firm's needs. Remember to send a personalized email or handwritten letter to every single person you interviewed with.

QUICK TIPS

- Research the company's website and prepare questions to bring to the interview.
- Bring copies of your résumé and writing samples.
- Dress for success.
- Sell your skills and know-how, but don't be full of yourself.
- Be knowledgeable, friendly, and positive.
- Ask questions about the company and the position.
- Send a thank you letter.
- Do not send social network invites to the people you interviewed with.
- Follow up with a phone call and/or email.
- Don't give up!

- Even if the people you interviewed with have been very friendly, do *not* send them Facebook, MySpace, or any other social network invites. Always keep your professional and private life separate.

- Finally, if you don't hear back from the HR department,

follow up a few days later with a phone call and/or email. Ask for feedback about your interview and whether your potential employer needs further information or references.

In the near future, the competition will be tough, but a little extra effort can, and will, go a long way. Remember, hiring has always been cyclical, so don't give up!

INTERVIEW TRACKER

DATE	COMPANY/ CONTACT NAME	THANK YOU	FOLLOW UP CALL/EMAIL

8. How do you dress for success?

To make a fabulous impression at a career fair, a professional association event, an interview or on the job, remember to follow these very simple tips:

For women

- Suits and dresses
- Blouses, skirts, sweaters, and vests
- Pant suits and slacks
- Dress sandals or shoes (flats or moderate heels)

Depending on your company's dress code policy, the following items could be unacceptable:

- Jeans (except on casual Fridays)
- Backless dresses
- Jogging suits
- Tank tops
- Spaghetti strap tops
- Sweatshirts
- Shorts, sweats, and leggings
- Sneakers or athletic shoes (except on causal Fridays) and flip flops

For men

- Suits (tie can be optional)
- Button-down shirts, jackets, sweaters and vests
- Slacks that complement the jacket

- Dress and casual shoes

Depending on your company's dress code policy, the following items could be unacceptable:

- Jeans (except on casual Fridays)
- Jogging suits
- Tank tops and sweatshirts
- Shorts, sweats, and other beach wear
- Sneakers or athletic shoes (except on casual Fridays) and flip flops

Especially when starting a new job, every little thing counts. Therefore, how you dress will show your supervisor how you see yourself and how you approach your new job. Remember, presentation counts. Using clean and simple lines and looking polished and professional will inspire confidence and will definitely make a great first impression. However, as there are a lot of people out there competing for a job, try to find something that will make you unforgettable. For example, instead of using classic colors for your suit—black, gray, or navy—opt for earthier tones, such as brown or rich blue. For women, colorful accessories or a beautiful bag are additional ways to stand out from the crowd.

QUICK TIPS

- Presentation counts.
- How you dress will show how you see yourself and how you approach your job.
- Dress as you want to be seen—polished and professional.

9. How do you make a great impression in the first weeks in a new job?

The first weeks in a new job can be terrifying. You just joined a new company; you are a new employee and a new team member. Everything seems unknown and complicated. However, this is also an exciting time. You just started a new adventure, and you will finally start your career and become independent.

You can take control over your new professional life and make a fabulous impression by following these tips:

- Have a positive attitude: be friendly and polite. Show your confidence by always shaking hands firmly.

- Communicate openly: listen and ask questions.

- Read the employee handbook carefully; take notes on all the systems and rules of the company and become an expert on the organization's policies.

- Come in early and stay a little late.

- Be prepared to do "small" tasks: you will be building your knowledge from the ground up, so show enthusiasm and be dedicated and flexible. Remember, a task is never too small; it's always part of a larger mission.

- Avoid office politics and gossip. You will be exposed to it sooner or later, but try not to contribute to it.

- Everyone conducts personal business on company time, but try to keep it to a minimum. Use your lunchtime to check your personal emails, make dinner reservations, or schedule doctor appointments.

- Be nice to administrative assistants: the person who answers the phone or files papers can determine the quality of your job. Remember, support staff will impact your job performance.

- Get involved with activities outside of work such as happy hours or other functions. However, be on your best behavior during these events. Even if your co-workers or supervisors are starting to get drunk, try to limit yourself to a one-drink maximum. Remember, you have to earn the right to act like a fool, so, at least for now, consider work functions as second interviews.

- Finally, work hard but also enjoy your first weeks.

QUICK TIPS

- Be friendly and polite. Shake hands firmly.
- Listen and ask questions.
- Become an expert on the company's policies.
- Come in early and stay late.
- Be dedicated and flexible: be prepared to do "small" tasks.
- Avoid office politics and gossip.
- Use lunch time for personal business.
- Be nice to support staff.
- Get involved with work functions, but be on your best behavior.

JOB
NOTES
NOTES
NOTES
JOB NOTES
NOTES JOB
NOTES
NOTES

10. How do you stay organized while juggling many tasks?

Nowadays, the nature of work involves juggling many tasks at the same time. Therefore, it is essential that you develop a system that helps you stay on top of things.

- From your very first day, pick a calendar system. For example, Outlook is a great tool that can integrate different aspects of your life: client-related meetings, assignments, deadlines, and personal activities. Use it religiously. If you are not familiar with it, speak up and ask for help. Remember, support staff impacts the quality of your job, and in this case the IT team in your organization can assist you. You can also sync Outlook with your blackberry, which makes it easier for you to be constantly aware of your meetings and projects.

- A to-do list is a must. Update it regularly either first thing in the morning or at the end of the day. An easy way to define and prioritize your tasks is the following:

  – Tasks A: Urgent *and* important

  – Tasks B: Important but *not* urgent

  – Tasks C: Routine tasks

  An ideal day will have mostly As and a handful of Bs and Cs. However, understanding which tasks are urgent, important, or menial is not easy. Remember, even top management sometimes struggles in selecting and defining assignments. Therefore, don't be afraid to personally speak to your managers and ask for help in prioritizing. Also, if you get pulled into an urgent project, get clarification from your managers on your priorities. If something then comes up that throws your day astray, the list may remain untouched all day long. If that happens, don't panic. Stay a little late and use the quiet time to finish the tasks that were not accomplished.

- Finally, remember to keep your team members up-to-date on the progress of your tasks. Being honest about your workload will help your managers reassign tasks if necessary and thus efficiently serve the client, which is the first priority.

QUICK TIPS

- Pick a calendar system and use it religiously.
- Update your to-do list regularly.
- Ask for help in prioritizing.
- If the to-do list remains untouched, stay late and use the quiet time to finish the tasks.
- Keep your team members up-to-date on the progress of your tasks.

11. How do you become a great team player?

Being a team player comes naturally to many twentysomethings. In fact, you are much more collaborative and open to new ideas than any other generation. However, for the most part, during your college career *you* were primarily responsible for what you did and how you were graded. It was *you* and the book, *you* and the exam. In the workplace, you will be able to do very little without the help or the participation of someone else along the way. Almost everything has a team element, and working in teams is challenging. You are not only responsible for your own work; you are accountable for the overall success of the group. In this context, your function exists to serve the bigger picture. Yet working in teams can also be highly rewarding: you can learn new things, work with new people, and contribute to the success of a big mission!

In order to be a remarkable team player

- Start by making sure you fully understand what is expected of you. If you think that you don't have the competence to accomplish the task/s, speak up and ask for help or resources. Remember, being honest about what you can and can't do is essential for the overall success of your team!

- When you start working on your assignments, take ownership of your piece of work, and give the best of yourself.

- Pay attention to the project timeline, and always keep your team members up-to-date on progress of your tasks.

- If a team member needs help, collaborate, and, if necessary, share your knowledge with the rest of the group. Work in partnership. A poor job in managing the relationships with your team members equals poor end results. Remember, you will only be rewarded when the entire mission is successfully accomplished! Therefore, from the beginning of your professional life make the effort to cultivate healthy and productive working relationships.

QUICK TIPS

- Fully understand what is expected from you.
- Be honest about what you can and can't do.
- Take ownership of your piece of work and give the best of yourself.
- Be attentive to the project timeline.
- Keep your team members up-to-date on progress of your tasks.
- Work in partnership.

12. How do you create a fruitful relationship with your boss?

Developing an effective working relationship with your supervisor is essential, not only for the advancement of your career, but also for your well-being at work.

- First of all, remember that the boss–subordinate relationship is not one-way. Your boss needs your help to accomplish the tasks, so accept your responsibility, and manage upward. The more you can help him/her, the easier it is to establish a healthy working relationship and the easier it is to get things done on a daily basis. You are in charge of meeting his/her needs and making his/her life easier, so take the initiative to regularly provide your supervisor with feedback and insight. Remember, you are new to the organization and therefore you can contribute with fresh and innovative ideas!

- Determine your boss' communication style. Should you send emails, make a phone call, or schedule a meeting when delivering news or updates on projects? Does your boss prefer details or succinct messages? Understanding your manager's preferred work style and adjusting yourself to it will strengthen your boss' confidence in you.

- If your boss is a baby boomer, he/she will most probably not be very comfortable with instant messaging, Twitter, Facebook, or other similar platforms. He/she will also spend less time giving clear guidelines or delivering constructive feedback. You will be working with someone that is very different from you, but this is an opportunity for you to share your creativity and your knowledge, and to take advantage

QUICK TIPS

- Make your boss' life easier.
- Manage upward—provide your supervisor with feedback and insight.
- Determine your boss' communication style.
- Share your creativity and knowledge and take advantage of your boss' many years of experience.
- Be honest when making mistakes.
- Be creative—find new ways to do things more efficiently.
- Keep your manager/s in the loop regarding accomplishments and concerns.

of your boss' many years of experience. You are in charge of meeting his/her needs, so no matter how difficult it might be to adapt yourself to your manager's communication style, you will have to work hard and deliver good results. Remember, always look at work as a learning experience and as an opportunity to improve your skills.

- Be honest. You are not expected to get everything right the first time, so talking through mistakes or asking for clarification will make you grow professionally and ultimately earn your supervisor's trust.

- Be creative. Follow instructions and execute what your boss needs you to do, but take the time to explore ways to do things more efficiently and share your findings with your superior. Don't be overly aggressive about it, but make your voice known.

- Finally, keep your manager/s in the loop regarding your accomplishments, observations, and concerns. The more you give and receive feedback, the more in sync you'll be at your annual performance review!

13. How do you get the most from a mentoring experience?

Mentoring initiatives are well established in many organizations. If your company has a formal mentoring program, participate fully. The program will give you the opportunity to be guided through the challenges that you will encounter and will allow you to build skills and obtain tools specific to your own development needs.

To get the most from this experience

- Set realistic expectations right away. Talk about what you want to get from the experience and what your top issues are.

- Be open to feedback, and accept constructive criticism. Remember, the mentor's role is to help you become a better worker.

- Be responsive and proactive. Your mentor is often busier than you are, so don't be afraid to initiate contact.

- Share your successes. Focusing on problems and how to solve them is an important part of the mentoring process; however, you can also learn from successes. Understanding how you or your mentor were extremely effective on a particular project can give you ideas on how to solve a present issue.

- Be professional and follow through on commitments.

- Be open and honest. Speak up if your mentor is doing

something that bothers you, such as initiating unreasonably frequent contact or not answering your questions. Remember, the relationship should be easy and mutually beneficial.

If your company does not provide a formal mentoring program, take the initiative to seek out a manager—preferably not a direct manager—that you admire and from whom you think you can learn professionally. Be proactive, ask for a time to meet with him/her, and present your request clearly. Ideally, a mentor is someone who is different enough from you that you can master new skills and develop professionally through the interaction.

QUICK TIPS

- Set realistic expectations.
- Be open to feedback.
- Be responsive and proactive.
- Share your successes.
- Be professional and follow through on commitments.
- Be honest. The relationship should be easy and mutually beneficial.

MENTORING
JOURNAL
JOURNAL
JOURNAL
MENTORING JOURNAL
JOURNAL MENTORING
JOURNAL
JOURNAL

14. How do you track your accomplishments?

Responsibilities and duties are important to assess one's career development. However, accomplishments will set you apart and ultimately contribute to the advancement of your career.

From the very first day at your job

- Start tracking your accomplishments in a notebook or in a database on your computer. How did you go above and beyond what was asked of you? What tangible evidence do you have of accomplishments? What are you most proud of? These are just a few questions that you can ask yourself to help you track your successes.

- If you have shown improvement in an area, document it; if you have fixed a problem, cite it. Think of your work as a living résumé.

> **QUICK TIPS**
>
> - Track your accomplishments from the beginning.
> - Think of your work as a living résumé.
> - Cite specific accomplishments during your six-month or annual reviews.

When it comes time for your six-month or annual reviews, having a record of the projects, initiatives, and challenges you have managed, and being able to cite specific accomplishments will be highly valuable! Keeping track of your out-of-the-ordinary accomplishments will help you justify whatever you are asking.

ACCOMPLISHMENT TABLE

DATE	NOTES

15. How do you prepare yourself and get the most out of annual performance reviews?

To get the most from your performance reviews, make sure you understand how your company manages reviews.

- Ask the HR manager or your supervisor if you will have a six-month review and/or an annual review. Will it be a 360-degree assessment process[1]? Who will be delivering the feedback? Is there an annual salary increase policy? Don't be afraid to ask these questions. It is important to understand and to be comfortable with how the company evaluates employees' performances.

- Generally, a company's performance review system includes a self-review form. If it doesn't, take the initiative to create a document that incorporates your perspective of

  – Projects, initiatives, and challenges you have managed/worked on throughout the year

  – Out-of-the-ordinary contributions. Because you have been tracking your accomplishments throughout the year, this should be an easy task

  – Goals for next year

---

[1] The 360-degree assessment and feedback is a process that collects performance information from multiple perspectives—supervisors, peers, and direct reports—to identify individual strengths and developmental areas. The person being reviewed is also asked to provide a self-assessment.

– Your strengths and areas of development

– General feedback (needs, concerns, etc.)

• During the feedback session, be prepared and professional. Your manager/s should have given you important feedback during the year, so this should mainly be the opportunity to discuss the future, not the

> **QUICK TIPS**
>
> - Make sure you understand how your company manages performance reviews.
> - Take the time to complete the self-review form. Be honest and thorough.
> - During the feedback session, be prepared, professional, and positive.
> - Don't be afraid to talk about money; but don't be greedy.
> - Clearly understand what the next steps are, such as new responsibilities, areas that need improvement, and so forth.

past. However, if your managers are not comfortable with delivering feedback, and you have not received any constructive criticism throughout the year, your annual review will be an overwhelming experience. Don't panic. Be professional and ask for clarification whenever an issue is misunderstood. This type of review is more challenging than the first one. However, be positive about it, and remember that this is a time for you to gain valuable information, and new ideas about how you can excel at your job.

- If your company has a known annual pay increase system (i.e. 3 percent for average performance, 7 percent for excellent performance), and you think you deserve more, make that clear during the feedback session. Keeping track of your out-of-the-ordinary accomplishments will help you justify what you are asking. This doesn't mean that you will get what you want, and it might be more difficult during economic turmoil, but a discussion about expectations will eventually get you there. Don't be afraid to talk about money. However, don't be greedy. Remember, this is your first full-time job; your salary is important, but even more so are the skills you have learned throughout the year.

- Finally, the session should finish on an encouraging note, with a clear understanding of your strengths, your areas of development and training, and your opportunities for new responsibilities and promotion.

16. How do you remain fair and objective when evaluating others?

If your company's performance review system is a 360-degree assessment process, you will inevitably be in the position of evaluating your peers and managers at some point. Although it's hard to review a friend's, supervisor's, or difficult co-worker's performance, you need to be fair and honest and remember that, ultimately, you are helping the person's career and advancement.

Consequently

- Be objective and use fact-based information to assess strengths and areas of development. However, don't base your review solely on recent events. Make sure you evaluate the work performance over the entire year.

QUICK TIPS

- Be fair and honest. By giving feedback, you are helping the individual's career and advancement.
- Be objective and use fact-based information.
- Make sure you evaluate the person's performance over the entire year.
- Don't use stereotypes or assumptions while assessing performance.

- Don't let the fear of hurting a friend's feelings or making a boss angry lead to a "dry" evaluation. Talk to your HR manager about the feedback you would like to share and ask for advice on how to best explain it.

- We all have preconceived perceptions about people. Make an effort not to use stereotypes or assumptions while assessing performance.

17. How do you make the most out of tuition programs?

Tuition programs are well established in many organizations. This perk is highly valuable, yet often overlooked by young people that have just finished college and are not in a rush to go back to school. However, these programs can be very interesting for young professionals that need to acquire specific skills related to their new responsibilities.

In order to make the most of a tuition program

- Make sure you fully understand the guidelines of this benefit. Are you eligible right away, or do you have to wait six months before taking advantage of this program? Does the company reimburse any type of continuing education or only classes that are related to job duties? Do they pay up front, or do you have to go through the class first, and get reimbursed after you pass? Also, remember that many companies demand the newly educated employee to remain at the workplace for a certain amount of time or else reimburse the company for part of the tuition paid. Usually, the information above can be found in the employee handbook. If not, the HR department can give you an overview of this benefit.

- Even if you can take advantage of this benefit from the very beginning, don't. The first few months in a new job are overwhelming. You are still trying to understand which areas you are comfortable with and which ones need improvement. If the company has a formal six-month review, this is the perfect time for you to discuss training needs with your managers. If the company does not provide a formal feedback session, be proactive: ask for an informal six-month review with your supervisors. Are you on the right track? What are your strengths? What areas need improvement? The answers to these questions will help you determine your training needs.

- Many of the skills you have learned in college, such as research, writing, presentation, and organizational skills, will be valuable in your everyday job. Nevertheless, the reality is that all of your abilities will be put to the test. Even a strong writer will need to refine his/her writing skills and sometimes completely change his/her writing style according to the company's expectations. So don't panic—many of the competencies that need work will improve as soon as you fully understand what the company expects from you.

- When do outside classes then become interesting? If your job requires you to use specific tools such as PowerPoint, Excel, or Adobe Photoshop on a regular basis, or if you are working in an industry that demands you know more about a precise topic—wine, employment law, podcasting, a foreign language—or a specific talent, such as public speaking, a tuition program comes into play. These are the type of classes you should take advantage of during your first year in the workplace. Remember, the objective is to show your supervisors that you want to acquire the skills to be more productive at work and do a top-notch job.

If your company does not have a formal tuition program, you will have to convince your employer to design a personal program. Your six-month or annual review feedback session might be good times to present your case and to explain why the training will benefit your work and the company in general.

QUICK TIPS

- Fully understand the guidelines of your company's tuition program.
- Wait until your six-month review to discuss training needs.
- Many of the competencies that need work will improve simply by understanding what your supervisors expect of you and then focusing on those areas.
- Be proactive—show your supervisors that you want to acquire new skills.

18. How can you resolve a conflict at work?

Conflict arises from differences. When individuals come together, their differences in terms of values, attitudes, and communication styles contribute to the formation of conflict. Therefore, sooner or later, you will be exposed to a conflict. It can be a small disagreement with a team member, an argument with a co-worker, or even a dispute with your boss. Not everyone gets along, and in your professional career you will eventually work with or for someone that you don't like. Big or small, conflicts have an impact on your well-being at work, and, consequently, dealing with them quickly and honestly will prevent some of the negative atmosphere that will arise no matter what.

There are many ways to resolve a conflict, and you will eventually find your own way of dealing with disagreements in the workplace. You must have already experienced conflict in your personal life, so think of how you have successfully handled those situations before. Below you will find some tips that will help you deal with these uncomfortable moments during your first year on the job.

- Communication is key. Be honest and open about the issue/situation. Explain your point of view clearly and make an effort to improve the situation. If this doesn't work, ask for help from your HR manager or your supervisor/s. Sometimes, you just need a third party's insight/involvement to make things better.

- Don't get too emotional. Try to step back and look at the

bigger picture. Is it really worth it to make a big deal about the issue? How can you make a compromise? What is a possible solution?

- Choose your battles. Understand when you need to confront the situation and when you need to ignore it. If the person you are having trouble with is a team member or someone with whom you interact on a regular basis, then this is an important relationship, and you need to quickly address the issue/situation. But if it is someone you rarely see or who is well-known for creating conflict, then it is best to politely ignore the whole situation.

- Be positive and show interest in making things better.

It is often very stressful to have a difficult working relationship with another employee, but by being open and honest about the situation, by staying positive and by making an effort to improve the relationship, the negative atmosphere should be transformed into positive energy.

QUICK TIPS

- Communication is key— be honest and open about the situation.
- Don't get too emotional.
- Choose your battles.
- Be positive.

19. When is it time to resign, and how do you evaluate a job offer?

There will be times during your first year that you will just want to run away and quit your job. It could be the result of a sudden problem, a conflict with a team member, a disagreement with your boss, the stress of dealing with complex issues much sooner than expected, or a growing to-do list that keeps you from spending time on personal interests outside of work. All of these events can increase your level of stress, and you may begin to feel overwhelmed and ready to find a different workplace. This could just be a rough patch as you learn to adapt to new responsibilities and more complex work. Therefore, take a step back and evaluate the situation.

- If you are overworked, talk to your HR manager and/or your supervisor/s and ask for help. Remember, being honest about your workload will help your managers reassign tasks, enabling you to work more efficiently.

- If you are not learning anything new or if you don't feel as challenged as expected or if you just don't like what you are doing, express your concern to your supervisor first. If things don't change and your need to escape is a feeling that has been a long time coming, then you are probably ready for a new opportunity.

Considering a job change is never easy. Below are some tips on how to handle this delicate situation:

- Your job search should not interfere with your everyday job. Even if you have decided to leave, you are still an employee and should therefore continue to work hard and deliver good results. Use the early morning, your lunchtime, and the evening to conduct personal business such as phone calls to recruiters, interviews with potential employers, online job searches, and so forth.

- When you receive a job offer, take some time to make your decision. Ask for feedback from your family and good friends. Carefully evaluate every single element: salary, benefits, office environment, company culture, and responsibilities. How will your job be different from the current one? One big piece of advice: don't be overly obsessed about an immediate increase in pay. Try to think long-term when you are making this decision. Don't just

QUICK TIPS

- Evaluate the situation. Are you just overworked, or do you really want to quit your job?
- Your job search should not interfere with your everyday job. Continue to work hard and deliver good results.
- Use your free time to talk to recruiters, go to interviews, and conduct online job searches.
- Carefully evaluate your job offer. Advancing your skill set should be your main focus.
- Don't burn bridges. Emphasize the positive when giving notice.
- Write a resignation letter.
- Ask for a letter of recommendation.

jump for the short-term financial incentive. Obviously compensation is very important, but advancing your skill set should be your main focus during your first years on the job.

- If you have decided to quit your job, then it's time to give notice. You don't want to burn bridges, so, while you are explaining your decision to your manager, emphasize how the company has benefited you but how it's time to move on. Offer to help your employer even after you are gone, via email or phone.

- Write a resignation letter and hand it to your HR manager. Find out about the benefits you are entitled to receive upon leaving (e.g. unused vacation time) and how to roll over your 401K.

- Before you leave, ask for letters of recommendation from your managers.

20. How can you stay healthy and relaxed while working hard?

Working hard, delivering good results, and showing that you are committed to your job are all very important during your first year in the workplace. Your supervisors will appreciate your enthusiasm, and your dedication will lead to positive changes—a better salary increase, a faster promotion, more responsibilities and so on. Therefore, prepare yourself to work hard and to come in early and stay late. However, this doesn't mean you have to completely sacrifice your personal and social life. Having personal interests outside of work is healthy, and it will make you more productive at your job.

- Find one or two things that you are passionate about and try to fit them in your day or your weekend. This could be a sport, a class, a charity, or it could be spending time with your family or good friends. Just make sure you have one or two activities that will help you unwind and relieve stress.

- Use your vacation time. In almost every workplace, you will lose your vacation time if you don't use it by the end of the year, so make sure to plan ahead and take advantage of your days off. Even though your starting salary won't allow you to go on vacation on a beautiful beach, you can definitely find ways to have fun and relax. Sometimes, taking a Friday off and exploring the city you live in or just taking some time for yourself will make you a much more productive employee the following Monday.

Also, if you are working hard and you are staying late in the office, you will probably start some poor eating habits. Eating

QUICK TIPS

- Find one or two things you are passionate about and fit them in your day or weekend.
- Use your vacation time.
- Eating well equals working well. Healthy food also provides energy for your non-work activities.

chips or chocolate because you don't have time for a proper meal, or skipping dinner because you worked late and then went out for drinks with friends are all very bad habits. Also you may want to spend your money on clothes, concerts, and drinks instead of good food. However, if you eat well, you will work well, and you will feel energized for your non-work related activities. So, here are some tips on how to eat better, even on a tight budget:

- Eat breakfast; it will keep you motivated and energized for many hours. Even on a tight budget, you have many options: milk and cereals, whole wheat bread and honey, or a fruit yogurt and granola are all healthy breakfast meals. You can bring all these items from home and stock them in your work refrigerator.

- Bring lunch from home. An omelet, pasta, or homemade sandwiches are all easy-to-make and healthy options that will allow you to eat well without spending too much money.

- Buy some snacks and leave them in the office. For example, dried fruits, nuts, cheese sticks, and yogurt are all inexpensive, but healthy, snacks.

- Don't skip dinner, especially if you will be drinking later in the evening. Make the effort to go home and prepare yourself a simple meal, or call in friends and cook dinner with them.

Choosing non-work related activities to relieve stress, enjoying your time off, and eating healthy foods are all equally important. By following these suggestions, you will have a fabulous and productive year!

INTERVIEWS

Five very different people have been interviewed for this book. Tamara is a Gen Y hard-working woman who entered the workforce in 2006. She is a contract coordinator in the business and legal affairs division of Sony Music. Etty is a bright young woman with four years of working experience under her belt. She struggled to find her career path, but she now has a true passion for what she does. She is a PR director, working on food and beverage accounts at RF|Binder. Erin doesn't have a typical career path. A year out of college, she became a partner in a small French-American training company and moved to Paris for a couple of years to help develop the business. She then created her own training company. Cartier North America became one of her clients, and, after a while, they offered her a job. She is now their training manager. Rob's career started at Arthur Andersen LLP. After only a year, he was promoted to manager. He then joined a start-up as a CFO for several years. The company ended up being sold. He later joined the mergers and acquisitions transaction work at Deloitte & Touche, and is now a director. Finally, Emanuele Grimaldi is a successful Italian businessman. After college, he joined the family business, the Grimaldi Group, one of the world's largest privately owned shipping companies. After a year of training, he was sent with his brother to the London office to develop the business. In a few years, they developed the biggest shipping line from the UK to West Africa and South America. He is a board member of many shipping associations, and is now managing director of the Grimaldi Group.

Tamara, Etty, Erin, Rob, and Emanuele are a diversified sample of professionals, a mix of people who have eclectic backgrounds and unique working experiences in various industries. I have asked each to look back at the beginning of their careers and provide me with some insight on what was challenging for them, how they overcame obstacles during those first years on the job, and what a young person should do and not do to best leverage his or her first working experience. For Tamara and Etty, it was a pretty easy exercise. They just had to go back a few years. For Erin, Rob, but mainly for Emanuele, it was a more complex process. Therefore, their insights do not only come from their own working experiences, but also from what they have observed and learned over the years.

In the next chapter you will find a synopsis of each interview. The full version of the interviews can be found at www.zeldafreud.com under myworkbook/book interviews.

TAMARA J. DEWS

Contract Coordinator, Business & Legal Affairs, Sony Music, a global recorded music company

- Favorite place to relax: Chelsea Piers and the Hudson River Park
- A person that you admire: My mom
- The thing that you do best: Multitask
- The thing that you do worst: Saying yes to everyone
- Favorite book: *I'm on My Way but Your Foot Is on My Head* by Bertice Berry
- 3 indispensable things: Honesty. Flexibility. Humility.

Tamara J. Dews is a contract coordinator, business & legal affairs with Sony Music Entertainment. In this role, Tamara manages all aspects of contract administration for her clients, including negotiating, drafting, and editing licensing and manufacturing agreements and issuing advance payments to third party record labels. Tamara holds an intellectual property law certification from New York University School of Professional & Continuing Studies and a Bachelor of Arts in history and politics from Mount Holyoke College.

IMPORTANT COMPETENCIES & HOW TO APPROACH THEM

Manage your time: Before I leave work each night, I make a to-do list of what I need to do for the next day. The next day,

I tweak it as needed. Whatever I don't complete, I add to the next day's to-do list. I also use Outlook for my meetings and personal business.

Write: Make sure that you write clearly and that the grammar is correct. Otherwise, it comes across as if you don't take your job seriously. I read my emails over before sending them out, and if I am writing an important memo I will have a co-worker or my boss look it over.

Manage your boss: Communication is key. You may not always like the people you work with, but it's not a popularity contest. It is about getting the job done in the most efficient way and delivering good results.

Supervise: I hire and supervise the interns in our department. A few things will make you a good supervisor: an open door policy, a balance of constructive criticism and praising, and the ability to give clear directions but also some freedom so that the person can find his/her own way of doing things.

DO

- Keep a list of your accomplishments. This is essential. I made sure I kept track of all my out-of-the-ordinary accomplishments and used that as a tool to show that I was doing a great job and that I deserved a very good raise. It really helped during my first year's performance review.

- Understand what you want to do in life. Try to work on as many projects as you can during your first couple of years of professional experience in order to fully understand what you want to do, what you are really good at, and what you don't like. Use your universal skills if you want to change industries. Highlight the things that you do well—the universal skills, such as planning skills and organizational skills. These can translate to any industry.

- Be flexible. Show that you don't just do your own job well but you can also take on other tasks and adapt to whatever comes your way. Show that you are committed and that you can handle many projects at the same time.

DON'T

- Don't rest on your laurels or ride on someone else's coattails. These things can help you get in the door, but only the work you produce is going to help you move ahead in your career. Make your mark.

- Don't embellish. Be confident about what you have to offer and what you can do. Going back to the universal skills, if you tell a potential employer, "I am a great planner, I planned this event, and even though it was in a different industry, it was a big success," shows that you are confident and you can deliver.

- Don't be modest. You have to be your own spokesperson. Even though I was keeping a list of my accomplishments, I was a little apprehensive in the beginning about presenting them. But talking about your successes is the only way for people to know how much you have accomplished.

Modesty is good when you are interacting with people on a personal level, but when you are a professional, you have to sometimes put the modesty aside and be your own spokesperson.

ETTY LEWENSZTAIN

Director, RF|Binder Partners,
a global communications management
agency of the Ruder Finn Group

- Favorite place to relax: Getting a massage or being in a yoga studio
- A person that you admire: My mom
- The thing that you do best: Cooking
- The thing that you do worst: Sometimes, a lack of confidence in my abilities
- 3 indispensable things: Honesty with yourself and others. Self-motivation. Family.

Etty Lewensztain is a director at RF|Binder who works on food and beverage accounts. She brings an extensive food and wine background to the company and has produced many large-scale wine-tasting events and exclusive seminars with high-profile wine authors, educators, and sommeliers. Having cooked at several Los Angeles restaurants, and having studied food journalism under prominent editors at *Food & Wine* and *Bon Appétit* magazines, as well as at the French Culinary Institute, Etty has forged valuable relationships with many food and wine industry leaders. Etty graduated from the University of Pennsylvania in 2004 with a BA in communications and a double minor in art history and Italian studies. She has also completed the certificate program in wine with an honors distinction at the International Wine Center in New York

City, and received accreditation from the American Sommelier Association in Viticulture and Vinification.

IMPORTANT COMPETENCIES & HOW TO APPROACH THEM

Manage your time: I use Outlook religiously and I make daily to-do lists. I usually have a to-do list for every account I am working on and a master to-do list with the most important priority stuff. I am very much into self-reminders too. I write post-it notes about everything—whether I have to buy a new toothbrush or write a PowerPoint. Reminding yourself of things and writing things down is very helpful.

Analyzing: During college you learn how to think about things, how to break down ideas in order to comprehend them, and how to create relationships between ideas. The development of these mental tools is one of the top takeaways from college, and I apply this skill a lot at work.

Manage your boss: People often think that the boss relationship goes one way, but it is really a two-way relationship. You are the boss to your boss and the boss is the boss to you. In the beginning, you will feel like you are the underdog, but in the end you will realize that your supervisor has a lot on his/her plate, and the more you can help him/her, the easier it is to establish a healthy working relationship and the easier it is to get things done on a daily basis.

Supervise: When you start supervising people, you sort of feel their pain because you know what they are going through. Sometimes people need to be held by the hand a little bit more, and sometimes you need to let them find their own way. If you try to micromanage them instead of leading them to the route where they can sort of self-discover, they will not learn the skills they need to. Supervision is also about showing people how to do a certain job or how to speak to a certain person, and then giving them some freedom to figure it out. Sometimes, because of deadlines and time restraints, it is almost easier to do things for people instead of showing them, but it is not the right way, and it means that you kind of have failed at your job.

DO

- Broaden your horizons. A lot of people try to pigeon hole themselves into "I'm a banker" or "I'm a lawyer" type and don't allow themselves the opportunity to learn something that they may not know they are into. It is very hard to know at your first job level what you are good at, what you are bad at, what kind of lifestyle you want to have. So keep your options open.

- Be ambitious. Be ambitious about your choices, reach out to long-shot opportunities, and be your own spokesperson.

- Make your boss' life easier. Do even more than what you are expected and even more than what you are assigned.

- Be creative. Many people just execute things or go through procedures and processes without finding more efficient ways to do something or better ways to create more interesting results. Be curious about new things and new ways of doing your work, and speak up whenever you find a credible idea—but don't overstep your boundaries.

DON'T

- Don't forget to spell-check your résumé , cover letters, and emails. Grammar errors and typos make you look terrible.

- Don't give up when times are hard. Don't let an adverse situation be a deal breaker.

ERIN CORRIGAN

Manager, Training & Internal Communication Department, Cartier North America, a jeweller and watch manufacturer that is a subsidiary of Compagnie Financière Richemont SA

- Favorite place to relax: On the beach with a book and some shade, or with a glass of wine at a bar with friends
- A person that you admire: My grandmother
- The thing that you do best: I understand and adapt to personalities quickly
- The thing that you do worst: Organize my personal finances
- Favorite book: *Eat, Pray, Love* by Elizabeth Gilbert
- 3 indispensable things: Music. Books. A pair of running shoes.

Erin Corrigan is the manager of the training and internal communication department at Cartier North America, a position she's had since January 2008. In this role, she and her team help increase employees' and partners' knowledge, confidence, and passion in the Cartier brand. Prior to working for Cartier, Erin was a partner of a French-American training company based in New York and eventually relocated to Paris. Upon her return to the United States, Erin started her own training company, which specialized in communication and presentation training as well as team building. Erin graduated in 2000 from Rutgers University with a BA in anthropology.

IMPORTANT COMPETENCIES & HOW TO APPROACH THEM

Present: When it comes to presenting, when you can't make it, fake it. If you don't feel confident, you have to pretend to feel confident because, if you don't, no one is going to believe in you and it is only going to get worse from there. Also, it is important to be nervous, but it's mainly about taking that nervous energy and making it pure energy. Presentations are "edutainment"—you are educating and entertaining at the same time. Therefore, have fun with your personality.

Analyze: Showing good analytical skills is crucial. Anyone can take orders and do what they are told to do, but you will shine much more than anyone else around you if you are capable of analyzing—coming up with options and thinking about the end result of those options.

Supervise: Understand personality types quickly and adapt your supervising style to those different personalities. Also, make people responsible for their own work and their own actions.

- Understand the value of work. Roll up your sleeves, work hard, and don't complain about it. You can hope to be recognized, but you shouldn't expect people to make a big deal about it. Remember, this is your first working experience.

- Be adaptable. When we talk about adaptability, it is almost anything—from the way you relate to people to your beliefs, the way you work, and the way you think. Instead of saying, "I don't know this," figure it out. You will grow and create new opportunities in your job if you are adaptable.

- Stay with a company as long as you are learning and growing. Once you are not learning and you have tried to seek opportunities to learn and they have not been given to you, then by all means, go. Hopping around for better offers, especially if you are in a small industry, is not a good idea.

- Be open-minded. Come in with your own set of beliefs, ideas, and ways of doing things, but accept that there are better ways of doing things. Be willing to learn.

- Make your boss' life easier. The easier you make your boss' job, the more you will be recognized. If you take on as much as you can, and you do your job correctly and effectively, you will be the star of the office.

DON'T

- Don't burn bridges—you just never know.

Director,
M&A Transaction Services,
Deloitte & Touche, one
of the largest audit and
consulting firms in the world

- Favorite place to relax: Cycling on a bike
- A person that you admire: My family
- The thing that you do best: Manage people
- The thing that you do worst: Making time for my personal interests
- Favorite book: *Atlas Shrugged*, by Ayn Rand
- 3 indispensable things: Health. Being mentally challenged in work and personal endeavors. Time with family.

Robert Rostron is a director in the Deloitte & Touche New York M&A Transaction Services practice with over twelve years of relevant public accounting and transaction related experience, serving both private equity investors and corporate clients in diverse industries. Prior to joining Deloitte, Robert was the chief financial officer of Energy.com, a start-up company he joined as the fourth employee. Prior thereto, he was a manager with Arthur Andersen LLP. Robert holds a BS in accounting and business with honors (magna cum laude) from the State University of New York at Albany. He is a certified public accountant and a member of the AICPA and the New York State Society of CPA's.

IMPORTANT COMPETENCIES & HOW TO APPROACH THEM

Present: Presenting is something I have always struggled with. My advice is the five P's: Prior Preparation Prevents Poor Performance. If you are not a natural public speaker, make sure you address that by preparing more.

Write: When you are submitting work, make sure you review it. Ask a peer to look it over as well. There is nothing worse than getting documents with grammar errors and typos all over the place. It is sloppy and it reflects poorly on the person.

Analyze: In order to analyze efficiently, stay on top of general business and news and know what's going on in the world at all times. Personally, I read the Wall Street Journal and the Financial Times every day. I also read online articles from the New York Times. Analyzing means knowing what is going on, what can go wrong, and then trying to mitigate that. You are not always going to be successful, but you can definitely try to manage risk.

DO

- Prepare, prepare, prepare. Just make sure you are prepared beforehand for whatever you are going to do.

- Understand what your boss is expecting from you. Ask for feedback—don't wait until your six-month or annual reviews. Ask for constructive feedback and build on that.

- Exploit your strengths and manage your weaknesses. Take advantage of the things that you do well, and, as you become a manager, surround yourself with people that are strong at what you are not good at. It is called working as a team.

- Look at the bigger picture. Understand what the goals are for the company and how what you are doing on a day-to-day basis fits into that. You may do something very well, but it may not fit into the big picture of what the company is trying to do.

- Have personal interests outside of work. Figure out one or two things that you are passionate about and work with them. It will make you more productive at work.

DON'T

- Don't be obsessed about immediate compensation. Try to think of a long-term perspective when you are making career decisions. Don't just jump for the short-term financial incentive.

Managing Director, Grimaldi Group, one of the world's largest privately owned shipping companies

- Favorite place to relax: In my house in Capri
- The thing you do best: Developing new projects
- The thing that you do worst: Administrative tasks
- Favorite book: *Karaoke Capitalism*, by Jonas Ridderstrale and Kjell Nordstrom
- 3 indispensable things: I try not to have indispensable things.

Emanuele Grimaldi is the managing director of the Grimaldi Group, one of the world's largest privately owned shipping companies. He joined the family business right after college and has been expanding the various lines of the Group ever since. He is the board member of many prestigious shipping associations such as the European Community Shipowners' Association. Emanuele holds a BS in economics and commerce with honors (summa cum laude) from the University of Naples, Italy.

DO

- Understand what your strengths are. Examine yourself and look at what your qualities are. Then do what you believe you can be really good at.

- Be passionate about what you do and go the extra mile. Today, the world has become extremely competitive. In business, the reference is not the national market anymore; it's the global market. Therefore, it's easier to be successful if you love what you are working on. However, even the most talented individual has to put forth a great degree of effort to move ahead. Even if you have fabulous ideas, if you only work 9 to 5, you won't see stellar results. So, be disciplined, work hard, and develop skills that will make you globally competitive!

- Be like a sponge. During your first couple of years on the job, try to absorb everything. Read a lot, and try to learn from every single person that works with you.

- Be humble. You can bring a lot of new and fresh ideas to a company. However, don't overstep your superiors or other older co-workers. If you are overly aggressive about your own set of ideas or beliefs, you might generate conflicts within the company, making your work life more difficult. Therefore, when making a contribution, be smart about when and whom you speak to.

- Be ambitious. Try to benchmark yourself to the best in the world. Always improve yourself.

CONCLUSION

Wayne Gretzky, a Canadian professional ice hockey player nicknamed "The Great One" and generally regarded as the best player in the history of the NHL, wrote in his autobiography:

> All I wanted to do in the winters was to be on the ice. I'd get up in the morning, skate from 7:00 to 8:30, go to school, come home at 3:30, stay on the ice until my mom insisted I come in for dinner, eat in my skates, then go back out until 9:00. On Saturdays and Sundays we'd have huge games, but nighttime became my time. It was a sort of unwritten rule around the neighborhood that I was to be out there by myself or with my dad.

Gretzky's impressive commitment of time on the ice and his genuine love for the sport—eating in his skates definitely demonstrates that—are what made him different from all the other players. His athletic abilities were not considered

In a nutshell, here are the top Do's for a twentysomething to best leverage his or her first year on the job:

1. Work hard and be ambitious. Work even more than expected and even more than assigned. Show that you can handle many projects at the same time, and always improve yourself.
2. Do what you are good at and what you are passionate about. Have big dreams.
3. Make your boss' life easier—it is a two-way relationship. Accept your responsibility and manage upward.
4. Be creative and anticipate needs. Read a lot and look at how what you do on a daily basis fits into the bigger picture. Then come up with ideas on how to do your work better or how to create more interesting results.
5. Review your work. Spell-check your résumé, your cover letters, and your emails.
6. Be loyal. Stay with a company as long as you are learning and growing. Don't be obsessed about immediate financial compensation.

impressive. It was his dedication, his passion for the sport, and his ability of thinking far ahead during the game that made him "The Great One."

The very best athletes are a great example of how, very often, it is not about how you are built: it is about your commitment, your hard work, and a passion for what you do that sets you apart. These elements relate very well with the many Do's and Don'ts that our interviewees have expressed. All five of them, from the youngest to the most experienced, have observed that hard work, ambition, and a genuine passion for what you do are essential ingredients to achieving success.

Finding the field you are good in and passionate about is definitely an important step, but you won't be great from day one. Success requires hard work, consistent practice, and a desire to always improve. Tiger Woods and the younger Michael Phelps, or Steve Jobs and Jeff Bezos are additional examples of how constant practice and a ferocious discipline are necessary ingredients to a successful career.

I hope MYWORKBOOK has given you a better understanding of the actual functioning of the workplace. You should now feel more empowered during your job search process, and more in control over your professional life.

Finally, as Steve Jobs once said, "We don't grow most of the food we eat. We wear clothes other people make. We speak a language that other people developed. We use a mathematics that other people evolved... I mean, we're constantly taking things. It's a wonderful, ecstatic feeling to create something that puts it back in the pool of human experience and knowledge." This is *your* time to make a difference, to use all of your talents and skills to stand out from the crowd and set an example! So, believe in yourself, work hard, and good luck!

MY TOP **TIPS**

Vladimir Horowitz, a legendary pianist, once said, "If I don't practice for a day, I know it. If I don't practice for two days, my wife knows it. If I don't practice for three days, the world knows it." Inspired by this quote, my top tips for those of you looking for a job or entering the workforce are:

1. Practice, practice, practice. Practice your interviewing skills, your writing skills, your presentation skills. Every little thing that we do in life or at work can be improved, so aim to get better and to constantly upgrade your skills. Remember, constant practice is the #1 rule for any type of success in life.
2. Do something you are passionate about. Don't just follow the trends of the moment.
3. Even if you work in a large company, think and act as an entrepreneur: be curious and creative about new ways of doing your work, and try to always think far ahead.
4. Manage up. Make your boss' life easier by going above and beyond the tasks assigned and by always maintaining a positive and enthusiastic attitude.

Dear Readers:

I hope MYWORKBOOK can bring the best out of you and make you shine like a star during interviews, career fairs, networking gatherings, and, finally, at *work*!

And I wish to stay in touch and help you even further in your career: visit **www.zeldafreud.com**! The site will be an additional resource during your job search and your first year in the workplace. It will display a blog and monthly interviews with professionals from different industries. So, log onto my website, and read about job hunting tips, office life and career trends. I hope to hear from you soon.

Zelda

About the Author: Zelda Freud is an HR Manager at RF|Binder, a New York City global communications management agency of the Ruder Finn Group. She was hired in 2006 to create the firm's HR structure, and is in charge of recruiting, professional development, annual 360-degree assessment processes, career management guidance and counseling in employee relations. Prior to her arrival in the U.S., Zelda was a Research/Teacher Assistant at the University of Geneva, Switzerland in the Faculty of Psychology and Human Resources. She was also a Project Manager at a Career Guidance institution in Geneva, developing career paths for young professionals and unemployed. She has a Bachelor's degree in Psychology and a Master's degree in Human Resources and Organizational Psychology from the University of Geneva. She also obtained a Master's in Media Ecology: Communication Studies from New York University. Zelda was born in Italy, and has lived in Milan, Paris, Panama City and Geneva. She now resides in Williamsburg, Brooklyn with her husband.

About Schools for Hope: Schools for Hope's mission is to build, maintain and staff schools in impoverished parts of the world and provide children with the fundamentals of learning including writing and simple mathematics. Additionally, Schools for Hope is building awareness to the growing problem of illiteracy and the need for basic education around the world as a solution to our many global problems.

BUY A SHARE OF THE FUTURE IN YOUR COMMUNITY

These certificates make great holiday, graduation and birthday gifts that can be personalized with the recipient's name. The cost of one S.H.A.R.E. or one square foot is $54.17. The personalized certificate is suitable for framing and will state the number of shares purchased and the amount of each share, as well as the recipient's name. The home that you participate in "building" will last for many years and will continue to grow in value.

Here is a sample SHARE certificate:

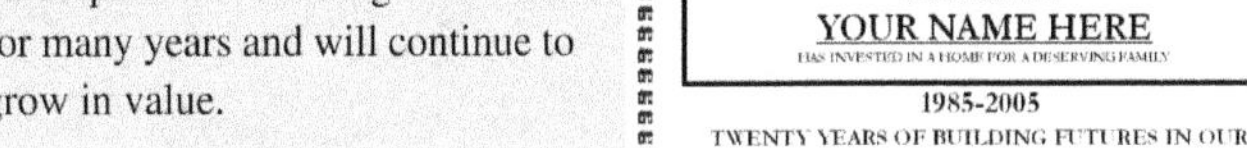

YES, I WOULD LIKE TO HELP!

I support the work that Habitat for Humanity does and I want to be part of the excitement! As a donor, I will receive periodic updates on your construction activities but, more importantly, I know my gift will help a family in our community realize the dream of homeownership. ***I would like to SHARE in your efforts against substandard housing in my community!*** *(Please print below)*

PLEASE SEND ME ___________ SHARES at $54.17 EACH = $ $___________

In Honor Of: ___________

Occasion: *(Circle One)* *HOLIDAY* *BIRTHDAY* *ANNIVERSARY*

OTHER: ___________

Address of Recipient: ___________

Gift From: ___________ ***Donor Address:*** ___________

Donor Email: ___________

I AM ENCLOSING A CHECK FOR $ $___________ PAYABLE TO HABITAT FOR HUMANITY OR PLEASE CHARGE MY VISA OR MASTERCARD *(CIRCLE ONE)*

Card Number ___________ Expiration Date: ___________

Name as it appears on Credit Card ___________ Charge Amount $ ___________

Signature ___________

Billing Address ___________

Telephone # Day ___________ Eve ___________

PLEASE NOTE: Your contribution is tax-deductible to the fullest extent allowed by law.

Habitat for Humanity • P.O. Box 1443 • Newport News, VA 23601 • 757-596-5553

www.HelpHabitatforHumanity.org

Printed in the USA
CPSIA information can be obtained
at www.ICGtesting.com
JSHW012043140824
68134JS00033B/3231

9 781600 375736